M000222386

CITY OF OXFORD
THROUGH TIME
Stanley C. Jenkins

AMBERLEY PUBLISHING

Christ Church College: The Meadow Buildings
Victorian buildings at Christ Church, designed by the Irish architect Sir Thomas Newenham Deane (1828–99), and completed in 1866.

First published 2012

Amberley Publishing
The Hill, Stroud
Gloucestershire, GL5 4EP

www.amberley-books.com

Copyright © Stanley C. Jenkins, 2012

The right of Stanley C. Jenkins to be identified as the Author of this work has been asserted in accordance with the Copyrights, Designs and Patents Act 1988.

ISBN 978 1 4456 0998 0

British Library Cataloguing in Publication Data.
A catalogue record for this book is available from the British Library.

Typeset in 9.5pt on 12pt Celeste.
Typesetting by Amberley Publishing.
Printed in the UK.

Introduction

Oxford is first mentioned by name in 912. The town was one of the 'burghs' or fortified places that King Alfred and his descendants had constructed to protect Wessex during the Viking wars. At that time, Alfred's son Edward the Elder and his daughter Aethelflaed were slowly, but inexorably, recovering English territory from the Danes. Aethelflaed was the widow of a Mercian nobleman who had been entrusted with the defence of London, and it is likely that she would have employed her father's engineers to lay out the new burgh at Oxford. Although there was already a minster church and a small pre-existing settlement in the vicinity, the new town was on an immeasurably greater scale, and for that reason Lady Aethelflaed can be seen as the founder of Oxford.

The burgh at the Oxen-ford was built in a strategic position at a crossing point on the River Thames. It was well-suited for defensive purposes, and was laid out between the subsidiary channels of the Thames and the River Cherwell. The surrounding marshes and low-lying areas provided natural defensive features and the burgh itself was encircled by stockades and stone-faced ramparts. To the west, a 'hythe' or wharf was constructed on the River Thames. This enabled the new settlement to be supplied from Reading and London. Despite a destructive Danish attack in 1002, this West-Saxon stronghold soon developed into a prosperous and thriving town.

The Domesday Book records that, in 1086, Oxford contained 'as well within the wall as without ... 243 houses which pay geld, and besides these there are 500 houses less 22 so wasted and destroyed that they cannot pay geld'. Additionally, there were 217 houses held by the king, bishops and other important people, together with a further 80 dwellings held by the priests of St Michaels or St Frideswides. From this documentary evidence, late Saxon Oxford must have contained around 900 houses and, assuming an average figure of five people per household, this would suggest a population of approximately 4,000.

Oxford became a recognised centre of learning during the twelfth century. As the number of students increased, hostels or 'halls' were opened to accommodate them, while benefactors began to found autonomous colleges, which tended to be much larger than the halls and were supported by endowments. It is estimated that there were, in the mid-fifteenth century, around seventy halls in Oxford, together with ten colleges. In time, further colleges were founded and many of the earlier halls were absorbed or converted into the new collegiate foundations. By 1852 there were nineteen colleges and five halls (including Magdalen Hall, which became Hertford College in 1874, and St Edmund Hall, which was incorporated as a college in 1957).

Oxfordshire was heavily involved with the Civil War, which began in 1642. The first large battle took place at Edge Hill, near Banbury, on 23 October. Although this engagement was inconclusive, it enabled the King to set up his wartime capital in Oxford. The city was extensively fortified by a sophisticated system of earthwork bastions, while at the same time the Royalists created an outer ring of detached outposts at places such as Woodstock Palace and Bletchingdon House. For the next four years Oxford was in a state of semi-siege, although the Parliamentarians made no attempt to storm the city, and on 24 June 1646 the Royalists surrendered without bloodshed.

The population of Oxford in 1801 was 11,694, rising to 37,057 by 1901, by which time the urban area had extended well beyond the confines of the original settlement. However, the main period of growth took place during the early twentieth century, when the city expanded in all directions, absorbing once-rural communities such as Headington and Cowley. The population had reached 80,540 by 1931, while in 2011 Oxford had an estimated population of 151,900.

Layout of the Book

The book is arranged in the following sequence, starting at the railway station and finishing with the River Cherwell:

1) From the Station to Carfax and along St Aldates.
2) Carfax to Magdalen Bridge via the High Street.
3) Merton Street, Turl Street and New College Lane.
4) Cornmarket, St Giles, Broad Street and Catte Street.
5) Parks Road and miscellaneous colleges.
6) Oxford railways.
7) Oxford buses and trams.
8) The rivers Thames and Cherwell.

Acknowledgements

Thanks are due to Graham Kew, Diana Lydiard, Michael French, Terry Walden, Ingram Murray and Bob Sheldon for help with the supply of photographs for this book. Other images were obtained from the Lens of Sutton Collection, the Soldiers of Oxfordshire Trust (*pages 10, 15 and 58*), the Oxfordshire Yeomanry Trust (*page 30*), and the author's own collection.

Lady Margaret Hall: The Wordsworth Building
Originally an all-female establishment, Lady Margeret Hall was founded in 1878. Margaret Thatcher and Benazir Bhutto both studied at this college.

Layout of the City: Carfax and the Four Ways

The streets of the Saxon burgh were laid out in a cruciform arrangement within the protective wall, and this basic town plan has survived until the present day. The crossroads at the centre of the medieval town became known as 'Carfax', or the Four Ways (*quatre voies*). The four thoroughfares were Cornmarket, St Aldates, High Street and Queen Street, which extended north, south, east and west respectively towards the long-demolished city gates. (*Right*) Carfax Tower, on the corner of Queen Street and Cornmarket, is the only remaining portion of St Martin's church, which was demolished in 1896. (*Below*) This Tudor map of Oxford is orientated from east to west; the city wall is clearly depicted, while Carfax is marked by a letter 'N'.

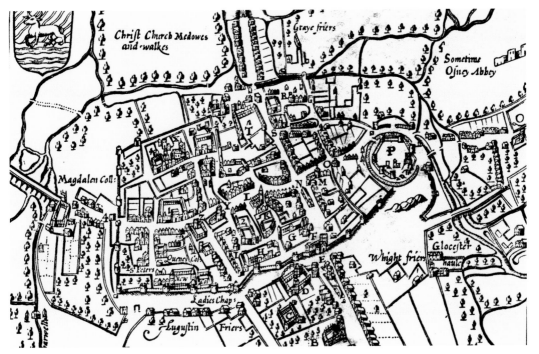

Park End Street: The Junction with Rewley Road

Present-day travellers arriving in Oxford by train can reach the city centre by walking eastwards along Park End Street – a locality that has experienced many changes over the years. The above photograph shows a group of old buildings at the junction of Park End Street and Rewley Road, including the triple-gabled Robin Hood pub and the four-storey Five Alls Inn, together with the Railway Hotel on the corner. (*Below*) These buildings were demolished around 1933 to make way for the Royal Oxford Hotel.

Park End Street

The south side of Park End Street, looking east, probably captured around 1919. The large building in the centre of the picture was Saunder's Furniture Repository, next to which was Hall's Oxford Brewery and Hayter's blacksmith's shop. The shadow visible to the left was cast by the now-demolished Railway Hotel. (*Below*) A recent view, looking west. The former furniture repository has survived and is now a conference centre, entirely surrounded by modern buildings.

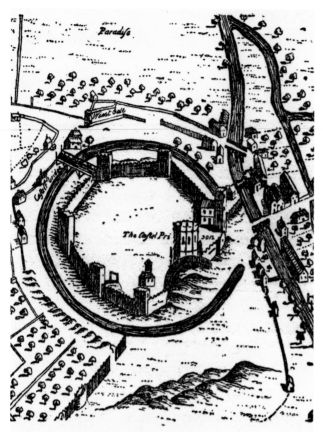

New Road: Oxford Castle

Forming a south-east continuation of Park End Street, New Road makes a junction with Queen Street, which in turn leads to Carfax and the city centre. Oxford Castle, to the west of New Road, was founded shortly after the Norman Conquest by Robert D'Oyly, who erected a motte-and-bailey castle – the 'motte', or castle mound, being some 250 feet in diameter. The castle buildings, originally of timber, were later replaced by permanent stone-built structures. (*Left*) A map surveyed by the pioneer map-maker Ralph Agas (*c.* 1540–1621) suggests that the castle was a roughly-circular fortress, with six mural towers and a tall stone keep on top of the castle mound. Most of the castle was dismantled after the Civil War, but a prison and county court were built on the site during the 1840s. (*Below*) The grass-covered castle mound remains a prominent local landmark.

New Road: Oxford Castle

Five of the castle's six mural towers have been destroyed, but St George's Tower remains extant. This grim-looking tower was at one time considered to be of late Saxon origin, while others have suggested, very plausibly, that it may have been erected by Robert D'Oyly during the tenth century to serve as a rudimentary keep, because the earth of the newly-raised motte was unable to bear the immense weight of a stone building. Although clearly of military origin, the tower also functioned as the bell tower of the long-demolished castle chapel. The upper view shows St George's Tower from the north, probably during the early 1920s, while the colour photograph, taken in 2012, shows the tower from the west.

9

Queen Street: The North West Frontier War Memorial

Situated at the junction of Queen Street and New Inn Hall Street, the North West Frontier war memorial was erected in July 1900. This commemorated members of the Oxfordshire Light Infantry who lost their lives during the Tirah Campaign against rebel tribesmen on the North West Frontier of India, between October 1897 and November 1898. The monument is in the form of an obelisk, and its foundations are no less than 20 feet deep. The memorial is inscribed with the names of sixty-two officers and men – most died of illnesses contracted during the campaign. The public open space around the memorial is now known as 'Bonn Square', and it has latterly been refurbished – as shown in the lower photograph.

St Aldates: Christ Church College & Cathedral

St Aldates, the busy thoroughfare running southwards from Carfax, contains a number of public buildings, including the post office and Town Hall, both of which are of Victorian origin and date from 1860 and 1893–97 respectively. The police station, further along the street, was built in 1936. The chief glory of St Aldates is Christ Church College (*above*), which was founded in 1525 by Cardinal Thomas Wolsey (1470–1530), who intended to build a magnificent new college on land that had formerly belonged to St Frideswide's priory. Several monasteries were suppressed to provide funds for the new college, which was to have an establishment of 180 persons, including a dean, 100 canons and 13 chaplains, together with public professors, teachers and choristers. The lower picture shows the college in 2012.

St Aldates: Christ Church College & Tom Tower

In the event, Cardinal Wolsey's grandiose building scheme was brought to an abrupt halt in 1529 when he fell from power. About three quarters of the great quadrangle had been built by that time, together with the largest hall and kitchen in Oxford. Tom Tower, at the entrance of Christ Church, and one of Oxford's most iconic buildings, is something of a hybrid. The gatehouse was built by Cardinal Wolsey, whereas the tower with its ogee cap was added by Sir Christopher Wren (1632–1723). Within the tower is 'Great Tom', a 6¼-ton bell that once hung in Osney Abbey. The upper view is a colour postcard, which was posted on 14 July 1917, while the lower photograph was taken in 2012.

St Aldates: Christ Church College & Tom Quad

(*Above*) Tom Quad, which measures 264 feet by 261 feet, is the largest quadrangle in Oxford. It has an unfinished appearance, insofar as the cloisters were never roofed-over and finished as Wolsey had envisaged. This postcard view, from around the 1920s, shows the western side of the quadrangle. (*Below*) The legend of St Frideswide and the Earl of Leicester, as depicted in a coloured postcard view dating from 1907 (*see next page*).

St Aldates: Christ Church Cathedral and the Shrine of St Frideswide

Cardinal Wolsey had intended to demolish St Frideswide's priory church and replace it with an entirely new college chapel, which would have been sited on the north side of Tom Quad. According to the seventeenth-century antiquary Anthony Wood, the Cardinal pulled down the west-end of the nave, 'containing almost half the body of the church, intending that the remaining part should serve only for private prayers'. At the time of the Dissolution of the Monasteries Henry VIII created six new Episcopal sees, one of these being the Diocese of Oxford, and in 1546 the truncated church of St Frideswide became Oxford Cathedral. An earlier plan, whereby Osney Abbey would have become the new cathedral, was rejected for financial reasons. The upper view shows the interior of the cathedral, looking east towards the altar, around the 1920s. Legend asserts that Frideswide, the patron saint of the city and university, was an eighth-century nun who rejected the amorous advances of Algar, the Earl of Leicester. Having fled into a deep forest, she prayed to God for help, and the Earl was, in consequence, struck blind when he tried to pursue her. Frideswide was thereby able to return to Oxford, where she became abbess of the priory that her father had founded. Frideswide died in 727. She was buried in St Mary's church, but her remains were subsequently re-interred in the priory church. The lower view shows her much-restored shrine, dating from about 1289, which can be seen between the Lady Chapel and the north choir aisle; its carved stonework depicts a wealth of luxuriant foliage – a reminder, perhaps, of the saint's flight into the forest.

St Aldates: Christ Church Cathedral and the Regimental Chapel

In 1929, it was suggested that a roll of honour be placed in the cathedral to commemorate the 5,878 members of the Oxfordshire & Buckinghamshire Light Infantry who died during the First World War. The idea was well-received and it was decided that the south choir aisle would be adapted for use as a regimental chapel, the new chapel being dedicated on 11 November 1931. The books of remembrance were subsequently updated to include the names of those who died in the Second World War. The upper picture shows the chapel in 1931, while the colour photograph was taken at one of the 'Page Turning' services that are held five times a year, and now include representatives of the Rifles and the Queen's Own Oxfordshire Hussars.

St Aldates: Christ Church Cathedral – An Exterior View

The cathedral, which also serves as the college chapel, forms an integral part of the collegiate buildings. Consequently, it is difficult to obtain an external photograph of this Anglo-Norman structure. The eastern end can be glimpsed from the college gardens and Christ Church Meadows, as shown in this postcard view of around 1955. The lower part of the tower is Norman, but the upper part, with its corner picacles and octagonal early-English spire, was added during the thirteenth century. The prominent 'rose window' was inserted by the Victorian architect Sir George Gilbert Scott (1811–78), who carried out a major restoration in 1870–76. The colour photograph was taken from Christ Church Meadows in 2012.

St Aldates: Christ Church College – The Meadow Buildings

The Meadow Buildings, to the south-east of Tom Quad, were constructed in 1862–66 at a cost of £22,000. The architect was Thomas Newenham Deane, who had also been involved with the design of the university museum, in conjunction with Benjamin Woodward (*see page 69*). The upper view is from a postcard, which was posted in 1914, and the lower photograph was taken in 2012.

Entrance to New Buildings, Christ Church, Oxford.

St Aldates: Pembroke College Gate Tower

Thomas Tesdale (1547–1610), a successful local businessman and former Mayor of Abingdon with interests in farming and the malt trade, bequeathed £5,000 to establish places at Balliol College for six scholars and seven fellows from Abingdon School. After many frustrating delays, however, the Tesdale Bequest was used to found Pembroke College on the site of the medieval Broadgates Hall. Additional funding was provided by Richard Wightwick, Rector of East Illsley in Berkshire, and the new college, which derived its name from the third Earl of Pembroke (who was then Chancellor of Oxford University), was opened in 1624. The college is situated to the west of Christ Church, the entrance and gate-tower being in Pembroke Square. The upper view, from an old postcard sent in 1907, shows the gate-tower from Pembroke Square, while the colour photograph was taken from the same vantage point in 2012. The crenellations have been removed and the ornate chimney-stack has been taken down, but otherwise few changes have taken place. Pembroke's most famous resident was the lexicographer Samuel Johnson (1709–84), who entered the college as a commoner in 1728 and lodged in a room on the second floor above the gateway during his short and unhappy sojourn at the college. He eventually left without taking his degree. However, in 1755 the university awarded him an MA in recognition of the work that he had undertaken in connection with his *Dictionary of the English Language*. At the end of his life, Dr Johnson donated his books to the college.

St Aldates: Pembroke College Chapel Quad

(*Above*) A further view from Pembroke Square, with St Aldates church to the right. Passing through the gate-tower one enters the Old Quad, which was built in the seventeenth century and remodelled in 1829–30. The much-larger Chapel Quad (*below*) contains an eighteenth-century chapel and a nineteenth-century Gothic hall, with tall windows and a projecting staircase tower. The architect was John Hayward of Exeter (1807–91), who may have based his design on the hall at Eltham Palace in London. The inset shows Chapel Quad, the buildings visible to the right contain fragmentary remains of the much-earlier Broadgates Hall.

NEW QUAD: PEMBROKE COLLEGE, OXFORD

High Street: Looking West

Returning to Carfax, it would now be convenient to describe Oxford's famous High Street, which extends eastwards in a great arc towards Magdalen Bridge, and contains two churches and the Examination Schools, together with many of Oxford's most famous colleges including All Souls, Brasenose, Queen's, Oriel, University College and St Edmund Hall. The upper photograph, from a sepia postcard of *c.* 1930, provides a general view of the 'High', looking west towards Carfax. University College can be seen to the left of the picture, while All Souls College, St Mary's church and Brasenose College are visible to the right, with the rotunda and spire of All Saints church in the background. The lower photograph, taken in 2012 from a position somewhat further to the west, provides a further glimpse of Carfax Tower.

High Street: St Mary the Virgin Church

Situated on the north side of the High Street, St Mary's is the university church and, as such, it has been the setting for many historic events – notably the show trials of the Oxford Martyrs Cranmer, Latimer and Ridley, which took place in 1554. Although the tower is thought to date from around 1320, much of the building dates from the fifteenth century; its architectural details are in the Perpendicular style. (*Right*) The Baroque south-porch, with its curious helical columns, was added in 1637. The architect was Nicholas Stone (*c.* 1585–1647), the son of a Devon quarryman who became a master mason and an accomplished sculptor. A general view of the church can be seen below, with part of All Souls College visible to the right.

High Street: All Souls College

All Souls College was founded by Archbishop Henry Chichele (c. 1362–1443) in 1438 as a college and chantry, in which masses would be said for the souls of those who had died during the Hundred Years War. The college was, in effect, a medieval war memorial. The college has three quadrangles, the earliest being the fifteenth-century Front Quadrangle, while the largest is North Quad, designed by Nicholas Hawksmoor (c. 1662–1736). The upper picture, from a sepia postcard of the 1920s, shows the west side of North Quad, with its Baroque gateway, whereas the colour picture provides a detailed study of Hawksmoor's distinctive 'twin towers' that dominate the eastern side of the quadrangle. The photograph was taken from the gateway that can be seen in the old postcard view.

High Street: Looking Eastwards from All Souls

A classic sepia postcard looking east towards Magdalen Bridge, probably around 1930, with Queen's College visible in the distance. The lengthy façade of All Souls College can be seen to the left of the picture. The main gate-tower, giving access to Front Quad, dates from the fifteenth century. A second gateway, which can be seen beyond the slight 'kink' in the façade, is part of a sixteenth-century extension. The colour photograph was taken in 2012.

High Street: Brasenose College

The original buildings of Brasenose College, known as the Old Quad, are entered from Radcliffe Street, but the college was extended south to the High Street during the nineteenth century. Brasenose was founded in 1509 by William Smith, Bishop of Lincoln (*c.* 1460–1514) and Sir Richard Sutton (*c.* 1460–1524), its name being derived from the old door knocker of Brasenose Hall, which had occupied part of the site. The upper picture, from an Edwardian postcard, depicts the Old Quad, which is overshadowed by the neighbouring Radcliffe Camera, while the colour view shows the High Street frontage.

High Street: Oriel College

Oriel College was founded in 1324 by Adam de Brome, Rector of St Mary's church, under the patronage of the ill-fated King Edward II. The college buildings incorporate three quadrangles, the hall, buttery and ante-chapel (*above*) being on the east side of Front Quad. The name Oriel is derived from a house known as La Oriele that stood on the site of the present-day college buildings. The colour photograph shows the college from Oriel Square.

High Street: The Rhodes Building

The upper view depicts a group of old buildings on the south side of High Street, including Long's cutlery shop and Mr Hedderley's sports outfitter's and tobacconist's shop. (*Below*) These premises were ruthlessly swept away during the early twentieth century to make way for an extension of Oriel College known as the Rhodes Building, which was built in 1908–11 and named in honour of the mining entrepreneur and African imperialist Cecil Rhodes (1853–1902), who left £100,000 to pay for its construction.

High Street: University College

Situated on the south side of High Street, University College can claim to be the oldest college in Oxford, having been founded by William of Durham in 1249. The upper picture shows part of the long and impressive façade of the college, which incorporates two periods of construction – the western end was built in the seventeenth century, while the eastern extension was added during the eighteenth century. The colour view shows the seventeenth-century building in 2012.

High Street: Looking Westwards

A general view of High Street looking west towards Carfax as depicted on a sepia postcard from around 1912. University College can be seen to the left of the picture, while the spires of St Mary the Virgin and All Saints churches rise above Brasenose and All Souls colleges on the right-hand side of the street. The recent view, taken from the centre of the street, shows St Mary's church, while Queen's College features prominently on the right-hand side of the picture.

High Street and Queen's College, Oxford

High Street: Looking East

(*Above*) The High Street, as shown on a postcard stamped with the date of 15 August 1913. University College is on the left and Queen's College can be seen to the right, while a horse-drawn tram makes its leisurely way along the single-track Oxford & District tramway. The Durham Building, on the extreme left, was built in 1903. Below is a modern view, taken from a similar vantage point, on the opposite side of the street in 2012. The tramway was closed in 1914, but Queen's College remains unchanged in the middle distance.

High Street: The Examination Schools

The Examination Schools, on the south side of the High Street, are of comparatively recent construction. They were designed by Sir Thomas Jackson (1836–1924) and opened in 1882. This impressive, Jacobean-style building was pressed into military service during the First World War, when it became the headquarters of the third Southern General Hospital – its capacious interior filled with hospital beds. The upper view is from a postcard sent during the First World War, while the colour photograph was taken in 2012.

High Street: Looking Westwards

An aerial view of High Street from Magdalen College Tower around 1912. The Examination Schools feature prominently in the centre of the picture, while Queen's College is visible to the right and the spire of St Mary's church can be seen in the background. The lower view, from a commercial postcard of around 1935, shows All Souls College and St Mary's church. A City of Oxford Motor Services Ltd double-decker bus stands in front of the college buildings, while a Great Western Railway dray horse can be seen in the foreground.

High Street: Queen's College

Queen's College was founded in 1340 by Robert of Eaglesfield, chaplain to Queen Philippa. Notwithstanding its medieval origins, the classical architecture of Queen's College dates mainly from the seventeenth and early eighteenth centuries. The façade of Front Quad, depicted on a sepia postcard of around 1912 (*above*), incorporates a Baroque gatehouse, which is flanked by the much taller gable ends of the east and west ranges to form a pleasing and symmetrical composition. The colour view was taken in 2012.

High Street: St Edmund Hall
St Edmund Hall originated
in the mid-thirteenth century
as a hall of residence for
undergraduates, but in 1957
it was granted a Charter
of Incorporation by Queen
Elizabeth II and thereby
became a conventional
college. In contrast to the
neighbouring Queen's College,
the buildings are small in
scale, and have an intimate,
domestic quality, as shown in
the accompanying views of
the North Quad.

High Street: The Junction with Longwall Street

The upper view, dating from around 1912, shows the junction of High Street and Longwall Street, while the lower view was photographed from a similar position a hundred years later. The corner building and the old cottages seen in the earlier picture have been replaced by a new and much larger building, which may incorporate part of the earlier structure, on the corner site. The Gothic building visible to the right is part of Magdalen College.

High Street: Magdalen College

Magdalen College was founded by William Patten of Waynflete in Lincolnshire (*c.* 1400–86), Bishop of Winchester, in 1458, the dedication being a reflection of the Bishop's devotion to St Mary Magdalen. Construction commenced in 1467 and the main buildings, including the Cloister and the famous tower, were completed by about 1509. The upper view, dating from around 1950, shows part of the High Street frontage, while the colour photograph was taken around sixty years later. The High Street frontage incorporates part of the Hospital of St John the Baptist, which predated the college, and had occupied part of the site. The large building that can be seen to the left in the upper picture is the college chapel, which forms part of the south range of the cloister.

High Street: Magdalen College

(*Left*) The Founder's Tower, which is on the west side of the Cloister, was the gate-tower of the original college buildings. It now forms a link between the Cloister and the adjacent St John's Quad. (*Below*) The main High Street gateway is a Victorian structure, erected in 1885 and replete with decoration, including statues of William of Waynflete, St Swithin and St Mary Magdalen. William of Waynflete, in a niche to the left of the doorway, is holding a model of his college, while Mary Magdalen, to the right of the doorway, is holding her emblematic jar of ointment. The buildings at the rear of the gateway, known as St Swithun's Buildings, were added during the 1880s. The architects were George Bodley (1827–1907) and Thomas Garner (1839–1906).

High Street: The Botanic Gardens

Sited on the west bank of the Cherwell, on the opposite side of the road from Magdalen College, the Botanic Gardens (*above*) were founded in 1621 by Henry Danvers, Earl of Danby (1573–1644). They are the oldest gardens of their kind in England. The gardens have three gateways, the main entrance, known as the Danby Gate (*below*) being a particularly exuberant Baroque structure. The statues represent King Charles I, King Charles II, and the architect Nicholas Stone who designed the three gateways.

High Street: Magdalen Bridge

The present Magdalen Bridge was built in 1772–78, although further work was carried out in the 1790s. The bridge, which has eleven arched spans of varying dimensions, was widened in 1882 to provide sufficient room for the Oxford & District Tramway Co.'s 4-foot-gauge tramline. The upper picture is from a postcard view of around 1930, while the colour photograph was taken in 2012. The latter image looks westwards along the roadway with Magdalen College tower featuring prominently in the background.

Merton Street: Merton College

Merton College is situated in Merton Street, which runs parallel to High Street. Christ Church Meadows are immediately to the south, and these classic Oxford scenes show the south façade of Merton College from the Meadows. The upper view is from a sepia postcard of around 1920, while the colour view was taken from the same vantage point in 2012. The college is the oldest in Oxford, having been founded in 1264 by Walter de Merton (c. 1205–77), Lord Chancellor and Bishop of Rochester.

Merton Street: Corpus Christi College

Like Merton, Corpus Christi College is situated in picturesque Merton Street. This college was founded by Richard Fox (*c.* 1447–1528), Bishop of Winchester, on 1 March 1517, with provision for a president, twenty fellows, and twenty scholars. The main gateway, which can be seen in this view from around 1900 (*left*), gives access to the Front Quad, which was built in the sixteenth century. The tall building that can be seen in the background is Merton College chapel. The colour photograph was taken in 2012 and, like the upper view, it is looking eastwards along Merton Street. Comparison of the old and new photographs will reveal that a new building has appeared to the east of Front Quad. This is the Thomas Building which, despite its traditional appearance, dates from the 1920s. The large building to the left of the picture is Oriel College.

Turl Street: Looking towards All Saints Church

Turl Street, a narrow side-street that connects the High Street with Broad Street, gives access to three colleges – Lincoln and Exeter colleges being on the east side, while Jesus College is on the west side of the street. The Edwardian colour postcard (*right*) is looking south towards All Saints church, on the corner of Turl Street. The church is now used as a library by Lincoln College. The lower photograph was taken from the northern end of the street in 2012. Exeter College can be seen to the left, while Jesus College can be seen in the middle-distance – the large, Gothic window is the east wall of the college chapel.

41

Lincoln College, Oxford

Turl Street: Lincoln College

Lincoln College was founded by Richard Flemming (c. 1385–1431), Bishop of Lincoln, who in 1427 received royal licence to unite the parishes of All Saints, St Michael at the Northgate, and St Mildred to form a 'little college of theologians' to combat the supposed 'heretical' teachings of John Wycliffe and the Lollards, who were questioning Catholic orthodoxy. St Mildred's church was demolished to make way for the new college, which has two quadrangles and a lengthy façade on the north side of Turl Street. The upper picture, from an Edwardian postcard, shows the Turl Street frontage in about 1912, while the colour photograph was taken a century later. John Wesley (1703–91), a graduate of Christ Church, was elected a fellow of Lincoln College in 1726. He received his MA in the following year and was ordained as a priest on 22 September 1728. His rooms in Chapel Quad are marked by a commemorative plaque.

Turl Street: Jesus College

Jesus College, on the south side of the street, was founded by Elizabeth I in 1571 as a result of a petition from Hugh Price (*c.* 1495–1574), the treasurer of St Davids Cathedral. This college has always been intimately connected with the Principality of Wales, and many of its students and most of its benefactors have been Welshmen. There are two main quadrangles, together with an additional range of buildings flanking Ship Street, which was added in the early twentieth century. The upper picture shows the interior of Front Quad in the 1920s, while the lower view shows the college from Market Street. In common with other Oxford colleges, Jesus College is associated with many eminent people – T. E. Lawrence (1888–1935) and former Prime Minister Harold Wilson (1916–95) are two of its most famous *alumni*.

43

Turl Street: Exeter College
Associated from its inception
with the West Country, Exeter
College was founded in 1314 by
Walter de Stapleton, Bishop of
Exeter, and re-founded by Sir
William Petre (1505/06–72) in
1566. Many of its buildings are
of seventeenth- or eighteenth-
century origin, but the chapel,
seen on the right of the upper
photograph, which was inspired
by La Sainte Chapelle in Paris,
was designed by Sir Gilbert
Scott and completed in 1860.

44

New College: The Medieval Gate-Tower

Despite its name, New College is in fact a very old institution, founded by William of Wykeham (c. 1324–1404), Bishop of Winchester, in 1379. The 'Great Quad' was completed by 1386, while the cloister and bell tower were added in 1400. The medieval gate-tower is situated in New College Lane – the archway visible to the right in the sepia postcard view, from around the 1920s, is a public right-of-way that connects New College Lane to Queen Street.

New College: Medieval & Victorian Architecture

In architectural terms, New College can be seen as the prototype for all later Oxford colleges, insofar it was built to a regular plan comprising a quadrangle, with a gate-tower, hall, chapel and library – this more or less standardised layout being similar to that of contemporary monastic foundations. Like other early colleges, New College features a range of monastic-style cloisters, which are shown in this postcard view of around 1912. New College has now expanded well beyond the confines of its original site, and the college includes nineteenth- and twentieth-century buildings, in addition to its medieval core. The lower view shows part of a long range of impressive Victorian Gothic buildings, which flank Holywell Street on the north side of the college.

New College: The City Walls

(*Above*) A substantial section of the city wall can be seen in New College gardens, and five open-backed bastions remain in situ (*see page 5*). These medieval defences were obsolete by the time of the Civil War – necessitating the provision of a complex system of earthwork defences, which formed an outer rim or perimeter, and extended well beyond the confines of the medieval city. (*Below*) The College's Holywell Street entrance looks south through the gate arch towards the medieval wall.

Cornmarket Street: St Michael at the Northgate

Oxford, St Michael's Tower

Returning once again to Carfax, we can now examine Cornmarket Street, Magdalen Street and St Giles. In historical terms, St Michael at the Northgate church, at the north end of Cornmarket, is of particular importance, insofar as its five-storey Anglo-Saxon tower is thought to have served as a defensive tower beside the north gate of the Saxon Burgh and, as such, it is the oldest building in Oxford. The upper view shows the tower from Cornmarket, looking north towards St Giles around 1930, while the lower photograph, which was probably taken during the late Victorian era, provides a detailed study of the north and west sides of this historic structure. The blocked doorway that can be discerned on the second floor must have given access to the wall walk at the top of the city wall.

48

Cornmarket Street: Looking North

The upper view is looking north along Cornmarket towards St Giles, *c.* 1900, with the Roebuck Hotel visible in the centre of the picture. Arthur Shepherd's tailor's shop and Goodhall & Sherratt's 'fancy repository', visible to the right of the Roebuck, were demolished around 1908 to make way for the Marlborough Chambers. Cornmarket, now a pedestrian precinct, is one of Oxford's busiest shopping streets, as shown in the lower illustration.

Cornmarket Street: Looking South

A further view of Cornmarket Street, this time looking north towards Carfax around 1912. The Roebuck Hotel again features prominently; this historic building was demolished after the First World War to make room for Oxford's first Woolworth's store. The recent photograph was taken in 2012 from a position further to the north, near St Michael at the Northgate church.

St Giles: The Martyrs' Memorial

Designed by Sir George Gilbert Scot, the Martyrs' Memorial was erected in 1841–43 to commemorate three Protestant bishops – Thomas Cranmer (1489–1556), Hugh Latimer (*c.* 1485–1555) and Nicholas Ridley (*c.* 1502–55) – who were burned to death during the reign of Queen Mary. As the flames were kindled, it is alleged that Bishop Latimer said, 'be of good comfort Master Ridley and play the man: we shall this day light such a candle by God's grace in England, as (I trust) shall never be put out.' Archbishop Cranmer, who had been persuaded to sign a recantation renouncing the Protestant faith, was burned five months later, famously holding his right hand in the flames and saying 'this hand hath offended'. His final words are said to have been 'Lord Jesus, receive my spirit ... I see the heavens open and Jesus standing at the right hand of God.'

St Giles: The Martyrs' Memorial & Balliol College

Two further views of the Martyrs' Memorial, looking south-east around 1955, and in 2012. The supposed site of the executions, which took place in the town ditch, just outside the city walls, is marked by a plaque in nearby Broad Street, although the exact location is much-disputed. Balliol College, which can be seen in the background, was founded around 1263 by John de Balliol (*c.* 1200–68) of Barnard Castle, the father of King John of Scotland, in penance for an attack on the Bishop of Durham.

St Giles: St John's College

St John's College, on the north side of St Giles, traces its history back to 1437, when Archbishop Chichele founded St Bernard's College as a college for Cistercian monks. The college was dissolved during the Reformation, but in 1555 it was re-founded by Sir Thomas White (*c.* 1550–1624), a prosperous London merchant. St John's has four quadrangles; the façade of Front Quad (*above*) is the former St Bernard's College, while North Quad (*below*) was added during the 1880s. The college's recent *alumni* include former Prime Minister Tony Blair.

St Giles: The Ashmolean Museum & Taylorian Institute

Founded by Elias Ashmole (1617–92), the Ashmolean Museum is the oldest museum in the British Isles, although the present building in Beaumont Street was not built until 1841–45; the architect was Charles Robert Cockerell (1788–1863). The eastern wing, facing St Giles, houses the Taylorian Institute, endowed by Sir Robert Taylor in 1788 for the study of modern languages. The figures that stand sentinel on top of the four detached Ionic columns represent France, Italy, Germany and Spain.

St Giles: The Randolph Hotel and the Great Fire of 1874

Designed by the Witney architect William Wilkinson (1819–1901), the Randolph is an archetypal Victorian 'grand hotel' in the Gothic style, with its main entrance in Beaumont Street. It is of yellow brick construction with stone dressings and a steeply-pitched hip-roof. The hotel was completed in 1864, although an extension was added in 1952. It is interesting to note that William Wilkinson spent his declining years in the Randolph – the unmarried architect having taken a suite of rooms in one of his finest buildings. The hotel narrowly escaped destruction on the night of 15 December 1874, when a major fire broke out in a neighbouring carriage-maker's workshops. Six fire engines were soon on the scene and an urgent request was telegraphed to the waterworks, but there was insufficient water-pressure for the hoses. Unchecked, the fire made astonishing progress, but Mr Blake, the Randolph's engineer, was able to run a hose from a large water tank at the very top of the building. With the aid of an engine, he was able to pump a jet of water onto the outside wall of the hotel and extinguish a small fire that had started in the window frame of Room 183. Meanwhile, policemen and volunteer firemen were rescuing people from the threatened properties – one unfortunate lady was so terrified that she had to be dropped from a first-floor window and caught in a 'jumping sheet' held by nine or ten men. The fire was finally extinguished about twenty-four hours later, by which time several shops and business premises had been gutted. The worst damage occurred in the carriage maker's yard – over 100 vehicles were destroyed.

St. Giles, S., Oxford

St Giles: Looking Southwards

Two contrasting views of St Giles, looking south towards Carfax. The upper view, showing Balliol College, is from an Edwardian colour postcard of around 1910, while the recent photograph was taken from a vantage point somewhat further along the street near St John's College. The historic college buildings have not changed, but the scene is now dominated by motor vehicles. The railings that can be seen in the postcard view mark the site of underground toilets, which have now been closed.

St Giles Fair and the 1830 Riot

St Giles Fair (*above*) is held each September on the Monday and Tuesday following St Giles Day. There was violent disorder at the fair in 1830, when forty-four anti-enclosure rioters, who had been arrested at Otmoor, were being escorted to Oxford Castle by the Yeomanry. Faced by an angry, jeering mob, the volunteer cavalrymen galloped away and their prisoners escaped. One brave sergeant (a former regular), who refused to flee, was pulled from his horse and severely beaten. (*Below*) The fair around 1972.

Broad Street: The Oxfordshire Militia

Broad Street runs eastwards from Cornmarket towards Parks Road and Catte Street. This Victorian photograph of around 1875 is from the Soldiers of Oxfordshire Museum and it shows members of the Oxfordshire Militia, drawn-up in formation outside Balliol College. The militia was a part-time reserve force that could trace its origins back to the Anglo–Saxon *Fyrd* that had defended Wessex during the Viking Wars. It was absorbed into the Territorial Force in 1908. Broad Street can be seen below, in 2010, with Balliol College to the left.

Broad Street: Balliol College

The immensely-long frontage of Balliol College extends from St Giles to Broad Street, the main Broad Street façade being in the Scottish Baronial style. The architect was Alfred Waterhouse (1830–1905). The college was originally intended to be a hostel for poor students, but it became a conventional college during the fourteenth century. Famous *alumni* include Prime Ministers Herbert Asquith (1852–1928), Harold Macmillan (1894–1986) and Edward Heath (1916–2005), together with the political economist Adam Smith (1723–90).

Broad Street: Trinity College

Built on the site of the much earlier Durham College, which was suppressed at the Reformation, Trinity College was founded in 1555 by Sir Thomas Pope (*c.* 1507–59), the son of an Oxfordshire yeoman who had risen to prominence as a Tudor civil servant and privy counsellor. Trinity has four quadrangles, its seventeenth-century chapel (*above*) being in the north-western corner of Front Quad. The Garden Quadrangle (*below*) has just three ranges. The north wing was designed by Christopher Wren.

Broad Street: The Sheldonian Theatre

The Sheldonian Theatre was funded by Archbishop Gilbert Sheldon (1598–1677) and designed by Christopher Wren, in order to provide a 'theatre', in which university ceremonies could be held. The building was formally handed over to the university in 1669. The upper picture, which was copied from an old 'magic lantern' glass slide, shows the Sheldonian around 1900, while the colour photograph was taken in 2012. The neighbouring Clarendon Building can be seen to the left in both illustrations.

Broad Street: The Clarendon Building
Designed by Nicholas Hawksmoor, this impressive structure was paid for by the profits of Clarendon's *History of the Great Rebellion,* which was written by Edward Hyde, first Earl of Clarendon (1609–1674), and published posthumously in 1702–04. The royalties were given to the university. The Clarendon Building was completed in 1715 and it was, until 1830, the home of Oxford University Press. The building, which is now used as offices by the Bodleian Library, features porticoes on its north and south façades. The monumental north portico (*left*) has detached Tuscan columns, whereas the corresponding portico at the rear has attached columns (*below*). The female figures that adorn the top of the building represent the nine muses – the present statues being fibre-glass replicas.

The Radcliffe Camera
Completed in 1749, the Radcliffe Camera derives its name from Dr John Radcliffe (1650–1714), who left £40,000 to erect a new 'Physic Library', and a further sum to pay the salary of a librarian. The architect was James Gibbs (1681–1754). The building has been used by the Bodleian as a reading room since 1860.

The Bodleian Library: The Schools
Quadrangle & Tower of Five Orders

The university library was originally
housed in St Mary's church, but in
the fifteenth century Duke Humphrey
of Gloucester (1391–1447) donated his
magnificent library to the university,
and the books and manuscripts were
then moved to a new home that had
been constructed for them above
the Divinity School – the new room
being known as 'Duke Humphrey's
library'. Sadly, the collection was
dispersed during the reign of Edward
VI, although the library was restored
by Sir Thomas Bodley (1545–1613)
and re-opened, with 2,000 books, in
1602. The Old Bodleian occupies a
group of historic buildings, including
the Schools Quadrangle, with its
celebrated Tower of Five Orders,
the Divinity School, Convocation
House and the Proscholium. The old
postcard (*above*) depicts the east side
of the Schools Quadrangle around
1912, while the recent photograph
provides a more detailed view of The
Tower of Five Orders.

The Bodleian Library: The Proscholium and the Divinity School

(*Above*) The entrance to the Bodleian is opposite the Tower of Five Orders, on the west side of the Schools Quadrangle. The bronze statue in front of the doorway is a representation of the Earl of Pembroke. The single doorway gives access to a vaulted entrance hall known as the Proscholium, which is situated beneath the 'Arts End'. Below is an Edwardian colour postcard view of the Divinity School. It is situated below Duke Humphrey's library, and can be entered via the Proscholium.

Oxford. Hertford College.

Catte Street: Hertford College & Hart Hall

Hertford was founded as a college in 1740, when Dr Richard Newton, the Principal of 'Hart Hall', which had been established by Elias de Hertford in 1284, obtained a charter of incorporation. Unfortunately, there were insufficient funds to sustain the new foundation, and the institution went into decline. The buildings were then taken over by Magdalen Hall. After many vicissitudes, Hertford College was revived by Act of Parliament in 1874; the necessary endowment was provided through the generosity of Thomas Baring (1831–91), a member of the famous banking family. Most of the Hertford College buildings are of Victorian or Edwardian origin, although the main quadrangle incorporates portions of the much older Hart Hall. The upper photograph shows the Catte Street façade around 1912, while the colour view provides a more detailed glimpse of the buildings on the far side of New College Lane, which form the North Quadrangle.

Catte Street: Hertford College & The Bridge of Sighs

The re-founded college was laid out by Sir Thomas Jackson in his usual English Renaissance style. The main quadrangle was built during the late nineteenth century, while the extension on the north side of New College Lane was added during the early twentieth century – the two parts of the college being linked by Jackson's famous 'Bridge of Sighs' (*above*). This well-known structure has become so much a part of the Oxford scene that it comes as something of a surprise to remember that the bridge was erected as recently as 1913. Although Hertford College is a relatively new foundation, it can claim several famous *alumni*, including Lord Clarendon, Charles James Fox (1749–1806), the philosopher Thomas Hobbes (1588–1679), and the Bible translator William Tyndale (*c.* 1494–1536) – all of whom had studied at Hart Hall or Magdalen Hall.

Parks Road: Wadham College

Wadham College was founded Nicholas Wadham (1532–1609) and his wife Dorothy (1534/35–1618) who, as his executrix, obtained a royal letter patent in 1610 and undertook all of the work that was required to bring the scheme to completion by 1613 when the new college was opened. The upper view shows the south side of the Front Quadrangle, around 1912, while the colour photograph shows the gate-tower and the west side of the Front Quad, which flanks Parks Road.

Parks Road: The University Museum

In 1847 Dr Henry Acland suggested that the University should establish a centre for the study of natural history, and the University Museum was duly constructed in 1855–60, the architects being Sir Thomas Newenham Deane (1828–99) and Benjamin Woodward (1816–61) of Dublin. The museum building, which features a large central gallery with a glass-and-iron roof, was extended in 1885/86 when the Pitt Rivers Museum was constructed, but the main frontage, seen here around 1912 (*above*) and in 2012 (*below*), remains more or less unchanged.

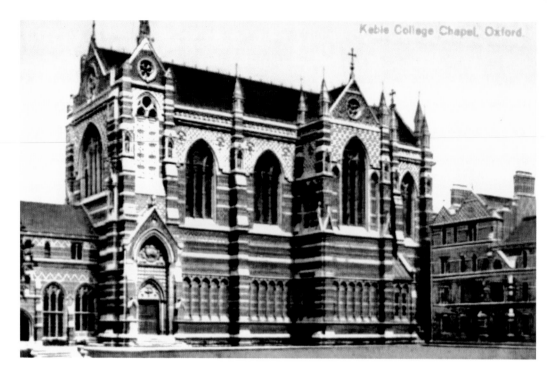

Parks Road: Keble College

Like the University Museum, Keble College, in Parks Road, is now regarded as an archetypal Victorian building. Designed by William Butterfield (1814–1900), and notable for its polychromatic brickwork, the college was formally opened by Lord Salisbury on 23 June 1870. There are two quadrangles, known as Pusey Quad and Liddon Quad, while a range of twentieth-century buildings have been added along Blackhall Road. The chapel, in Liddon Quad, shown around 1912 (*above*) and in 2012 (*below*), is particularly striking.

Norham Gardens: Lady Margaret Hall

Women were first admitted to Oxford in the 1870s, although they could not become members of the university until 1920. Lady Margaret Hall and Somerville, the first ladies' colleges, were founded as hostels for Anglican and Nonconformist students respectively, and they both became full colleges in 1960. Men were first admitted in 1979. Lady Margaret Hall boasts some surprisingly grand buildings in the Queen Anne style, including the Talbot Block, shown in a 1950s postcard view (*above*) and in a recent photograph taken in 2012 (*below*).

Mansfield Road: Harris Manchester College

Oxford and Cambridge had traditionally been exclusively Anglican institutions – Nonconformists being barred. This prohibition led to the establishment of various 'dissenting academies', including Manchester College, which was founded in Manchester in 1786 and moved to Oxford in 1889. Manchester became a hall of the university in 1990, and in 1996 it was granted a Royal Charter, thereby becoming a constituent college of the University of Oxford. Although justifiably proud of its Nonconformist and specifically Unitarian origins, the college is now open to mature students of all denominations. The college buildings in Mansfield Road were designed by the Manchester architect Thomas Worthington (1826–1909) and are of traditional appearance. This can be seen in the Edwardian postcard view and in the colour photograph, which was taken in 2012. The tall building with the Oriel windows is the college library.

Oxford. Worcester College.

Worcester College: The Eighteenth-Century Buildings

Situated in Worcester Street, at some distance from the other historic colleges, Worcester College received its charter in 1714 after Sir Thomas Cookes (1648–1701), a Worcestershire baronet, had bequeathed £10,000 to the university, with the aim of founding a college for students from his native county. Work commenced in 1720, but the construction of the college was a curiously-protracted process, and building operations were still under way during the 1790s. (*Above*) The Worcester Street façade has a slightly forbidding appearance – the projecting wings being not unlike the bastions of a fortress. (*Right*) Incessant traffic makes photography both dangerous and difficult, but this recent colour view nevertheless provides a view of the south wing and the recessed central portion with its Baroque pediment. The architectural style is reminiscent of the work of Nicholas Hawksmoor, who is thought to have been involved with the design of the building.

Worcester College: The Remains of Gloucester Hall

Worcester College was built on the site of Gloucester Hall, which had been established in 1283 as a school for Benedictine monks. Some of the medieval buildings have survived. The south side of the quadrangle (*left*) is of fifteenth-century origin. These picturesque old houses were associated with particular monasteries – the arms of Pershore, Glastonbury and Malmesbury abbeys being among those emblazoned above the doorways of each house. The lower view shows the south side of the medieval range. In the inset, an Edwardian postcard illustrates the medieval buildings at Worcester College.

Oxford Station

When opened on 12 June 1844, the Oxford branch had terminated in a small station in St Aldate's. The present station was brought into use on 1 October 1852, when the Oxford to Birmingham main line was opened throughout. The upper view shows a suburban train alongside the down platform around 1939, while the lower photograph shows the down-side station building in 1970. These timber-framed buildings were swept away as part of a major reconstruction scheme that was carried out in 1971.

Oxford Station: The Southern Approaches

Approaching Oxford from the south, the railway crosses over the Thames and then passes the site of former goods sidings on the up-side. Beyond, trains pass beneath the Osney Lane footbridge and enter the station. The footbridge provides a panoramic view of the southern approaches to the station, as shown in these contrasting photographs, one of which dates from 1971, while the other was taken in 2012. Beckett Street Goods Yard, to the right, has now been replaced by a car park.

OXFORD. 1/6/35.

Oxford Station: The North End

The upper picture, dating from 1935, shows a Witney branch train in the down-side bay platform, which was now been removed. (*Below*) Semaphore signals were a feature of the railway scene for many years, as exemplified by this 1970 photograph, which shows the northern end of the platforms, with Oxford Station North Signal Box visible to the right. This entire infrastructure has now been swept away, the only recognisable feature being the distinctive tower of St Barnabas' church.

OXFORD G.W.R. 18/6/1911.

Oxford Station: The Up-side Buildings

The main up-side station building boasted an extensive range of accommodation, including a booking office, waiting rooms, refreshment room, parcels office, stationmaster's office, telegraph office, mess rooms and toilets. The up- and down-sides of the station were linked by an underline subway, and lengthy canopies were provided on both sides. The upper photograph shows the up-side buildings in 1911, while the lower view illustrates station approach in 2012. Trees and foliage hide the present-day station building, which was built in 1990. The inset is part of the present-day station building.

Oxford Station: The Down-side Buildings

Facilities on the down platform included further waiting rooms and staff accommodation, together with a separate down-side booking office. The upper picture shows the down-side buildings in 1971, with the Victorian buildings still extant, whereas the lower photograph, taken in 2012, reveals a totally different scene – the only recognisable features being the trees. The modern building seen on the right is the Oxford Youth Hostel, which was opened in 2001, and is conveniently sited for those arriving in the city by train.

Oxford Station: Rewley Road

Oxford once had two stations, Rewley Road, to the east of the GWR station, being the terminus of a 30¼-mile London & North Western Railway branch from Bletchley. Opened on 20 May 1851, the station was designed by Sir Charles Fox (1824–1912) and built of pre-fabricated ironwork and timber. The structural components were identical to those employed by Messrs Fox & Henderson when they built the Crystal Palace. (*Below*) The site is now occupied by housing developments and the Saïd Business School.

Oxford Buses & Tramways

Modern visitors may be surprised to learn that Oxford once had a 4-foot-gauge tramway system, the City of Oxford & District Tramway Co. having been formed in 1879. The first line was opened from the railway stations to Cowley Road via Park End Street, Carfax and High Street, on Thursday 1 December 1881, while a second route was brought into use between Carfax and the Banbury Road in 1882. The upper picture shows a double-decker tramcar in the High Street, while the lower view shows Car No. 9.

Oxford Tramways: Demise of the System

The Walton Street branch was opened from St Giles to Leckford Road on 15 July 1884, and a line from Carfax to Lake Street, via Cornmarket and Folly Bridge, was added in 1887. The network was completed in 1898, when the Banbury Road line was extended to South Parade. (*Below*) Electrification schemes were opposed by 'conservationists' who objected to the use of overhead wires and, by the beginning of the twentieth century, postcards were portraying the horse-drawn trams as obsolete relics of the Victorian age.

Oxford Buses & Tramways

In 1906, the City of Oxford Electric Traction Co. was formed with the intention of electrifying the tramway, but local opinion had turned against the trams and the system was abandoned in 1914. The tramway company thereby became a motor bus operator, and the name 'City of Oxford Motor Services' was adopted in 1921. The upper view shows AEC Renown double-decker bus No. 368 at Oxford station in 1972, while the lower view depicts a present-day Oxford bus beside Queen's College.

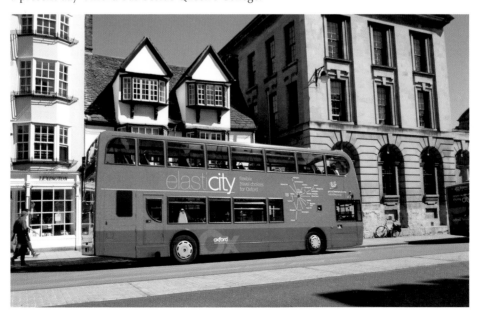

Oxford Buses & Tramways

Nationalisation in 1969 was followed by privatisation in the 1980s, the result being a fragmented industry in which the Oxford Bus Co. operates the city services, while Stagecoach has acquired the rural routes. The upper picture, showing a Regent bus at Oxford station in 1971, provides another reminder of the traditional maroon and purple-brown Oxford bus livery, while the Scania bus in Banbury Road (*below*) illustrates the current Stagecoach gold livery. The bus in front is an electro-diesel vehicle, in environmental green.

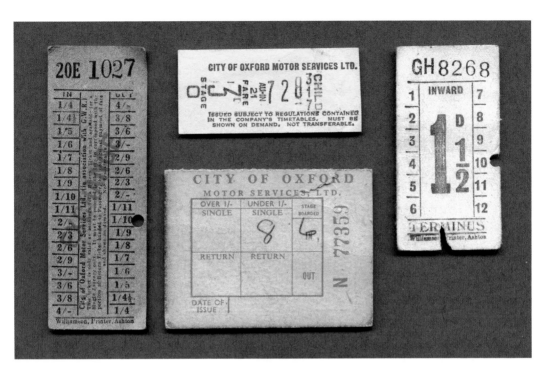

Oxford Buses & Tramways: Miscellany

(*Above*) Oxford buses and trams have utilised several ticketing systems over the years, including traditional 'punch' tickets that were issued by conductors from portable 'racks', and machine issues such as the Setright ticket shown here. At one time, tickets were printed on different coloured paper, according to fare values, although machine-issued tickets were normally green or yellow. (*Right*) Many Oxford tramcars ended their days as hen-houses and garden sheds, including this example, which was found on a farm at Yarnton and subsequently transported to East Hanningfield, in Essex, in connection with an abortive preservation attempt.

The River Thames: Looking South from Folly Bridge

The Thames has been navigable for centuries, and in medieval times the river was regarded as a major artery of communication for stone, timber and other heavy consignments. Oxford was a busy inland port, its importance being further enhanced by the construction of artificial waterways during the eighteenth century – the Thames was linked to the Midlands via the Oxford Canal and to the River Severn via the Thames & Severn Canal; both of these waterways were completed by 1789. The upper picture shows an animated scene on the river to the south of Folly Bridge, around 1912. The ornate wooden craft along the east bank were the luxuriously furnished and elaborately decorated college barges that functioned as floating boathouses and clubrooms. (*Left*) The barges have now been replaced by conventional boathouses sited further downstream, leaving an empty river bank, with a clear view of Christ Church Meadows.

The River Thames: College Barges

A further view of the college barges, moored stem to stern along the east bank of the river, around 1912. Many of these distinctive craft had been built locally by Messrs Salter of Folly Bridge. The colour view, which was taken from the cabin roof of the narrow boat *Towy*, provides a more recent view of the same stretch of river, looking north towards Folly Bridge. The tree-lined banks are just the same, but the college barges have disappeared from the scene.

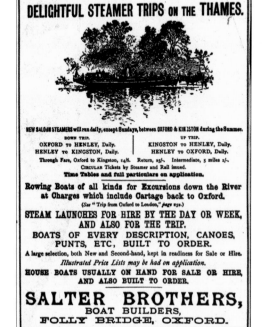

The River Thames: Salter's Steamers
Salter Brothers, the famous Oxford boat-building firm, was founded by John and Stephen Salter in 1858. Salters' commenced their Thames steamer service in 1888, the first steamer being the *Alaska*, which had been built at in 1883 by Horsham & Co. of Bourne End. The service ran from Oxford to Kingston, as shown in the accompanying handbill (*left*). The 91½-mile journey was accomplished in two days, with an overnight stop at Henley-on-Thames. Passengers were able to embark and disembark at locks or other recognised stopping places, and light refreshments were served aboard the steamers – although, as the Salters were a Methodist family, alcohol was not available. The upper picture shows the steamer *Henley*, which was built for Salter Bros by Edwin Clarke & Co. of Brimscombe in 1896. She was sold in 1976 and now works in the London area between Westminster, Kew and Hampton Court.

The River Thames: Salter Bros' Steamers

Salter Bros were probably at their peak during the 1950s, when seventeen vessels were in operation. Thereafter, the steamer service went into relative decline, and by the 1970s, the Oxford to Kingston service had been replaced by a number of short-distance trips, including half-day excursions from Oxford to Abingdon, and from Marlow to Henley-on-Thames. The upper picture shows the *Wargrave* forging upstream on the approaches to Oxford in the summer of 1974, while the lower picture shows the *Sonning*, as depicted on the cover page of the 1974 Salter Bros' timetable. The *Wargrave*, built by Salter Bros in 1913, has an overall length of 84½ feet, and she can accommodate 199 passengers. The *Sonning*, 85 feet overall, was slightly older, having been built by Salter Bros in 1902 and converted to diesel operation in 1947. She was sold in 1982 and is now working on the River Trent.

RIVER THAMES
PASSENGER SERVICES
1974

SALTER BROS. LTD.
FOLLY BRIDGE
OXFORD

The River Thames: Salter Bros' Jetty

Two views of Salter Bros' jetty at Folly Bridge. The upper view shows the motor vessel *Mary Stuart* alongside the jetty in 1974 while the lower view, taken in 2012, shows the *Mary Stuart*, tied-up alongside the *Lady Ethel* and the *Leila*. It is interesting to note that the *Mary Stuart* was originally a Dutch vessel known as the *Kagerplas*. Although colloquially-known as a 'steamer', the *Mary Stuart* is diesel-powered. With a length of 68 feet she can accommodate 162 passengers.

The River Thames: Historic Vessels at Folly Bridge

(*Above*) The hotel barge *Guidance*, seen at Folly Bridge in 1974, was a motorised Humber keel that had originally been equipped with a single square sail. (*Below*) Salter Bros' steamer *Goring*, photographed in 2012, was built by Salter Bros in 1913. She is 85 feet overall and can accommodate 199 passengers. All of these former Salter steamers are now listed on the National Register of Historic Vessels.

The River Cherwell

The tranquil River Cherwell, Oxford's slow-flowing 'other river', joins the Thames about a quarter-of-a-mile to the east of Folly Bridge, and is navigable as far as Islip, about 7 miles upstream. The lower part of the river flows past Christ Church Meadows, under Magdalen Bridge and alongside the University Parks. The riverbanks are attractively landscaped, as shown by these photographs of the 'Cherwell Walks'. One was taken during the early twentieth century and the other in 2012.

The River Cherwell: Parson's Pleasure and the Rollers

About 2 miles from Folly Bridge, the river is obstructed by a weir, and those wishing to proceed further upstream must haul their punts out of the water and propel them manually along a gently-inclined set of 'rollers', which lead to the upper reach. Until 1991, Parson's Pleasure was the site of an open-air, male-only bathing place that was much frequented by nude bathers and, to prevent embarrassment, ladies were asked to disembark and walk along a special path that skirted the area behind a high fence! The upper view shows a punt approaching the Rollers, probably around 1900, while the colour photograph was taken in the summer of 2012. It is difficult to believe that this idyllic rural location is a little under three quarters of a mile from the bustle and incessant traffic of Carfax!

The Cherwell, Oxford.

The River Cherwell: The Upper Reach

Once past the Rollers, the river becomes wider and deeper as a result of the constraining influence of the weir. This Edwardian coloured postcard provides an idealised impression of the river during the early years of the twentieth century, while the lower view shows a group of sixth-formers from Witney Grammar School on a punting trip during the 1970 summer vacation. Two of the party were about to start their first terms at university.

The River Cherwell

(*Above*) A further view of the upper reach near the Rollers. Many punters end their journeys at Marston Ferry Road, where the Victoria Arms provides a convenient resting place and turn-around point before the downstream trip back to Oxford. However, intrepid voyagers can press on towards Water Eaton, or even Islip, although the upper reaches are sometimes blocked by fallen trees or other navigational hazards. (*Below*) A lone punter shoots the central arch of Oxford Bypass Bridge some 4 miles from Folly Bridge.

Envoi

Two final views of the historic and beautiful City of Oxford. Tom Tower, Magdalen College Tower and the Radcliffe Camera are generally considered to be Oxford's three most famous buildings, and it would therefore be fitting to conclude with a last glimpse of the Radcliffe Camera, photographed from the south in 1975. Like all medieval cities, Oxford has its share of narrow alleyways and back-streets, many of which lead off from the busy High Street. The lower view shows the eastern end of Merton Street, looking west towards Oriel Square. Although taken in 2012, at the height of the summer tourist season when the city's main streets were thronged with people and traffic, this quaint old street was more or less empty.